P9-CMA-840

CREATIVITY IN BUSINESS

A Practical Guide for Creative Thinking

Carol Kinsey Goman, Ph.D.

A FIFTY-MINUTE™ SERIES BOOK

CRISP PUBLICATIONS, INC.
Menlo Park, California

CREATIVITY IN BUSINESS
A Practical Guide for Creative Thinking

Carol Kinsey Goman, Ph.D.

CREDITS
Editor: **Michael G. Crisp**
Designer: **Carol Harris**
Typesetting: **Dharma Enterprises**
Cover Design: **Carol Harris**
Artwork: **Ralph Mapson**

Copyright © 1989 by Crisp Publications, Inc.
Printed in the United States of America

Distribution to the U.S. Trade:

National Book Network, Inc.
4720 Boston Way
Lanham, MD 20706
1-800-462-6420

Library of Congress Catalog Card Number 88-72254
Goman, Carol Kinsey
Creativity In Business
ISBN 0-931961-67-X

This book is printed on recyclable paper with soy ink.

TO THE READER

According to a recent survey, when senior managers were asked to state the most important and valued traits in workers, they said *creative problem-solving and new ideas.* In business, creativity can help you launch major projects or untangle minor snafus. It provides a fresh insight and new perspective on even the most routine elements of your job. Best of all, it enables you to view problem-solving as a creative opportunity!

Sound like magic? While it can work wonders for you, creativity isn't some mystical force or extraordinary talent possessed by the lucky few. Rather, creativity is an ability everyone (to one degree or another) has. Even better, it is also a skill you can develop more fully.

This book was designed to help you uncover more of your innate creative potential, and then develop techniques that will allow you to "tune in" to your creativity at will.

Each section of *Creativity In Business* leads to a better understanding of how to become a better idea generator and innovative problem-solver. The sections are:

Section I — GETTING STARTED
Section II — CREATIVITY BLOCKS AND BLOCKBUSTERS
Section III — TECHNIQUES FOR IDEA GENERATION
Section IV — GROUP CREATIVITY
Section V — INNOVATION AND PRACTICAL SOLUTIONS

Learning to use more of your creativity will allow you to rekindle that spark of excitement about work, to be more confident in your ability to confront situations with fresh ideas and more innovative solutions, and to take advantage of the creative input of others.

Get set for a wonderful journey as you explore your personal creative talent. And good luck as you develop this ability into results-producing actions!

Carol Kinsey Goman, Ph.D.

Carol Kinsey Goman, Ph.D.

ABOUT THIS BOOK

Creativity In Business is unlike most books. It stands out from others in an important way. It's not a book to read — it's a book to use. The unique "self-paced" format of this book and its worksheets encourage the reader to get involved and try some new ideas immediately.

The objective of this book is to help those in business to develop and utilize more creative ability in their daily work. Using the simple yet sound techniques presented can make a dramatic difference in one's personal and professional success.

Creativity In Business (and the other books listed in the back of this book) can be used effectively in a number of ways. Here are some possibilities:

— **Individual study.** Because the book is self-instructional, all that is needed is a quiet place, some time and a pencil. Completing the activities and exercises will provide valuable feedback, as well as practical ideas you can use immediately on the job.

— **Workshops and seminars.** The book is ideal for assigned reading prior to a workshop or seminar. With the basics in hand, the quality of participation will improve, and more time can be spent on concept extensions and applications during the program. The book is also effective when it is distributed at the beginning of a session, and participants "work through" the contents. (For information on in-house seminars that elaborate on this material, see the box at the bottom of the page.)

— **Remote location training.** Books can be sent to those not able to attend "home office" training sessions.

There are other possibilites that depend on the objectives, program or ideas of the user. One thing for sure, this book will serve as an excellent source for review and future reinforcement.

ABOUT THE AUTHOR. Author, keynote speaker and seminar presenter, Carol Kinsey Goman is a nationally recognized authority on developing creative potential and applying it to business. Her client organizations include AT&T, Bank of America, American Society for Association Executives and the U.S. Chamber of Commerce.

For information on the *Creativity In Business* seminar contact Carol Kinsey Goman, Ph.D. at Kinsey Consulting Services, P.O. Box 8255, Berkeley, California 94707. (415) 943-7850.

CONTENTS

SECTION I: GETTING STARTED

What is Creativity?

Years ago in the newspaper column of Ripley's "Believe It or Not", the following item appeared: A plain iron bar is worth $5.00. If you take that iron bar and forge horseshoes from it, the value increases to $10.50. If it is made into needles, the price rises to $3,285.00. And if you make watch springs from it, it then is worth $250,000.00. Ergo, the difference between $5.00 and $250,000.00 is creativity.

"The human mind, once stretched to a new idea, never goes back to its original dimension."

Oliver Wendell Holmes

Definitions

- *Creativity:* Bringing into existence an idea that is new to you.

- *Innovation:* The practical application of creative ideas.

- *Creative Thinking:* An innate talent that you were born with *and* a set of skills that can be learned, developed and utilized in daily problem solving.

- *Creative People:* Those people who do not block their innate creativity and who focus their ability in various aspects of life.

All Of Us Can Enhance the Creativity We Possess

You Already Are Creative

In what areas of life do you display your creativity? (Hobby, work, relationships, public speaking, art, music, crafts, etc.)

_____

_____

_____

_____

Where have your creative ideas been put to practical use? (Party you hosted, report or project you designed, unique approach to a presentation, etc.)

_____

_____

_____

_____

What was the most creative thing you did as a child?

_____

_____

_____

_____

Where in your life would you like to apply more creativity?

_____

_____

_____

_____

What people (living or dead) are or were creative in ways that impressed you?

_____

_____

_____

_____

YOUR I.Q. (INTELLIGENCE QUOTIENT) IS NOT YOUR C.Q. (CREATIVITY QUOTIENT)

The late Dr. Richard Feynman was one of the world's leading theoretical physicists. After being awarded the Nobel Prize in Sweden, he flew to his old hometown and stopped at his old high school. While he was there he looked up his grades. They were not as good as he had remembered, so he asked to see his I.Q. score. It was 124—only slightly above average. He was delighted. "Winning a Nobel Prize is no big deal," he reportedly told his wife, "but winning it with an I.Q. of 124 is really something!"

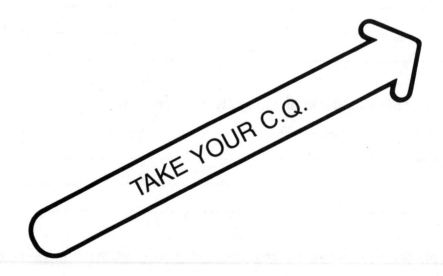

How High Is Your C.Q.? (Creativity Quotient)

Take the following self-test to check your Creativity Quotient. Score 3 for always, 2 for sometimes, 1 for once in a while, 0 for never.

_2_   1. Are you curious? Are you interested in other people's opinions, problems from other departments, customer feedback?

_2_   2. Are you a "creative opportunist?" Do you find opportunities for solving problems, creating wants, filling needs?

_2_   3. Are you a strategist? Do you spend time redefining your goals, revising plans to reach them or creatively using organizational changes to correct your own course?

_3_   4. Are you a challenger? Do you examine assumptions, biases, or preconceived beliefs for loopholes and opportunities?

_2_   5. Are you a trend spotter? Do you actively monitor change in your field such as technology, government regulations, or new management strategies to spot opportunities early?

_2_   6. Are you a connector or adaptor? Do you keep your eyes peeled for concepts you can borrow from one field to apply to another?

_3_   7. Are you a risk taker? Are you willing to develop and experiment with ideas of your own?

_2_   8. How's your intuition? Do you rely on your hunches and insights?

_3_   9. Are you a simplifier? Can you reduce complex decisions to a few simple questions by seeing the "big picture?"

_0_   10. Are you an "idea seller?" Can you promote and gather support for your ideas?

_2_   11. Are you a visionary? Do you think farther ahead than most of your colleagues? Do you think long term? Do you share your vision with others?

_3_   12. Are you resourceful? Do you dig out research and information to support your ideas?

_2_   13. Are you supportive of the creative ideas from your peers and subordinates? Do you welcome "better ideas" from others?

_2_   14. Are you an innovative networker? Do you have colleagues with whom you share creative ideas for feedback and support?

_1_   15. Are you a futurist? Do you attend lectures or read books about the "cutting edge" in your field? Are you fascinated by the future?

_2_   16. Do you believe you are creative? Do you have faith in your good ideas?

_33_ | SCORE |

CHECK YOUR SCORE USING THE SCALE ON THE NEXT PAGE

Score Your C.Q.

A score of 41–48 shows you have a very high creativity quotient. You will find creative ways to put the techniques in this book to use! 36–40 shows you're mentally ready to explore more of your creativity, and should do very well using the techniques and exercises presented. 30–39 indicates that you have yet to discover your true creative capacity. By practicing some of the ideas in the book you should be greatly encouraged by the positive results. Below 29 you may be surprised by the increase in your creativity after using this book. You don't know yet how creative you can be!

The self-test on page 5 was adapted from *An Honest Day's Work: Motivating Employees To Give Their Best,* by Twyla Dell. For order information, see the list in the back of the book.

SECTION II: CREATIVITY BLOCKS AND BLOCKBUSTERS

You Were Born to Be Creative

In the late 1940's, a group of psychologists were discussing the lack of creativity in most adults. They speculated that by the age of 45, there was only a minute percentage of the population who could think creatively. To prove that assumption they designed a creativity test and gave it to a group of 45 year olds. Less than 5 percent of them were judged creative by the test.

They continued testing by reducing the age of the subjects. They tested at ages 40, 35, 30, 25, and 20 years old. The 5 percent creativity figure stayed basically the same for all these groups. Finally at 17 years old the percentage of creative individuals rose to 10 percent. At the age of 5, it sky rocketed to over 90 percent! The conclusion? Almost everyone is highly creative at age five.

Benefits From Enhancing Your Creativity

Place a check in those squares for each statement that you believe to be true for you.

Increasing Your Creativity at Work Can:

☑ Help you make the best use of your talents, aptitudes and abilities.

☑ Enhance the enjoyment of your job.

☑ Cause you to have more self-confidence.

☐ Cause you to be a more valuable employee.

☑ Enhance your opinion of yourself as a proficient problem solver.

☐ Ultimately increase your income.

☐ Cause you to become more self-motivated.

☑ Help you to feel more innovative and "intrapreneurial."

☐ Give you a greater sense of control and mastery over your job.

If you checked even one box, it should motivate you to learn techniques presented in this book to increase your C.Q. (creativity quotient).

Blocks to Creativity

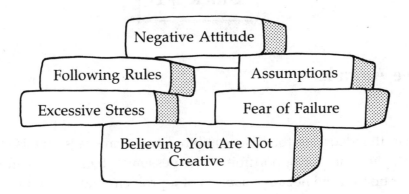

- Negative Attitude
- Following Rules
- Assumptions
- Excessive Stress
- Fear of Failure
- Believing You Are Not Creative

Creativity Blockbusters

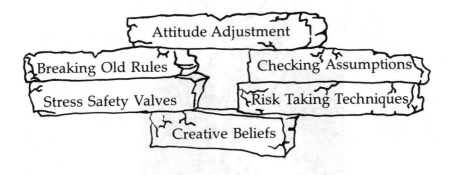

- Attitude Adjustment
- Breaking Old Rules
- Checking Assumptions
- Stress Safety Valves
- Risk Taking Techniques
- Creative Beliefs

**Discover What Blocks Your Creativity — Then Develop
A Blockbusting Strategy!**

Block #1

Negative Attitude

In Chinese, the ideogram for crisis combines two characters; one is the symbol for danger, the other for opportunity. The pessimist, by nature, will turn his or her attention on the negative aspects of a problem and expend creative energy worrying about possible detrimental outcomes. The optimist on the other hand will liberate creativity by focusing on the inherent opportunities.

WHAT IS YOUR ATTITUDE?

Blockbuster #1

Attitude Adjustment Scale

Please rate your current attitude. Read the statement and circle the number where you feel you belong. If you circle a 10, you are saying your attitude could not be better in this area; if you circle a 1, you are saying it could not be worse. Be honest.

	HIGH (Positive)	LOW (Negative)

1. If I were to guess, my feeling is that my boss would currently rate my attitude as a: .... 　10 9 8 7 ⑥ 5 4 3 2 1

2. Given the same chance, my co-workers and family would rate my attitude as a: .... 　10 9 ⑧ 7 6 5 4 3 2 1

3. Realistically, I would rate my current attitude as a: .... 　10 9 ⑧ 7 6 5 4 3 2 1

4. If there were a meter that could gauge my sense of humor, I'd rate a: .... 　10 9 8 ⑦ 6 5 4 3 2 1

5. My recent disposition — the patience and sensitivity I show to others — deserves a rating of: .... 　10 9 8 7 6 ⑤ 4 3 2 1

6. My attitude about my own ideas and creativity is: .... 　10 9 8 7 6 ⑤ 4 3 2 1

7. My attitude toward other people's creative ideas is a: .... 　10 9 8 7 6 ⑤ 4 3 2 1

8. Lately, my ability to generate lots of possible solutions has been a: .... 　10 9 8 7 6 ⑤ 4 3 2 1

9. I would rate my enthusiasm toward my job during the past few weeks as a: .... 　10 9 8 7 6 5 4 3 2 ①

10. I would rate my enthusiasm about my life in general to be a: .... 　10 ⑨ 8 7 6 5 4 3 2 1

TOTAL _____

A score of 90 or over is a signal that your attitude is "in tune" and no adjustments seem necessary; a score between 70 and 90 indicates that minor adjustments may help; a rating between 50 and 70 suggests a major adjustment; if you rated below 50, a complete overhaul may be required.

This scale was adapted from *ATTITUDE: Your Most Priceless Possession*, by Elwood N. Chapman. For order information, use the list in the back of this book.

Block #2

Fear of Failure

Fear of failure is one of the greatest inhibitors of natural creativity, and yet, every successful innovator has failed often. Tom Watson, Sr., the founder of IBM, was often quoted as saying, "The way to accelerate your success is to double your failure rate." Tom Peters, the current management guru, declares that the prescription for dramatically speeded-up innovation is dramatically increased rates of failure. Those who embrace failure as a by product of creativity, definitely have the advantage!

Blockbuster #2

Risk-Taking Technique

1. What is one creative risk you are currently considering?

2. Why is it important for you to take this risk?

3. If you took this risk and failed, what is the worst possible outcome?

4. If this approach failed, what are your other options?

5. How do you plan to deal with this failure?

Case History #1 — Fear of Failure

A woman in her thirties, Vicky was being groomed by her father to take control of the family business. Vicky told her best friend: "This is such a wonderful opportunity. I have so many new ideas about how to improve the business. I only hope that I don't let him down!"

The friend replied: "What would happen if you tried your best and still failed to meet your father's expectations? What if he didn't like your ideas?"

Startled, she replied, "Why, I'd feel perfectly awful!" Then her friend asked: "What would you do after you felt awful?"

Vicky verbally wound through an entire sequence of reactions. She fantasized leaving the area, changing her name, and finally joked about putting herself "up for adoption." At last she smiled and said, "I guess I'd have to find a way to survive".

Based on her response, do you think Vicky is a creative person?

☑ YES   ☐ NO

14

Block #3

Excessive Stress

Psychologically, an overly stressed person finds it increasingly difficult to maintain objectivity and has trouble perceiving alternatives. This is often accompanied by a great sense of pressure based on feelings such as not enough time, too many demands, or being trapped. The arousal of such distressful emotions will usually result in poor creative thinking and reduced decision-making abilities.

Blockbuster #3

Safety Valves for Stress

Place a check in the appropriate column. Rate yourself candidly.

Do very well 5	Average 3	Need Improvement 1	I am succeeding at:
	✓		1. Taking responsibility for my own stress. (not blaming others)
✓			2. Knowing my optimum level of stress. (where you do your best)
	✓		3. Balancing work and play.
	✓		4. Loafing more. (learning when it's appropriate to do nothing)
	✓		5. Getting enough sleep.
	✓		6. Refusing to take on more than I can handle.
✓			7. Exercising regularly.
		✓	8. Setting realistic goals.
		✓	9. Practicing relaxation exercises.
	✓		10. Taking pleasure in the here and now.
	✓		11. Valuing family and friends.

Blockbuster #3   (continued)

Do very well 5	Average 3	Need Improvement 1	
	✓		I am succeeding at:
	✓		12. Managing my time and setting priorities.
✓			13. Taking time for recreation and hobbies.
	✓		14. Avoiding too much caffeine.
✓			15. Emphasizing good nutrition in diet.
✓			16. Avoiding alcohol or other chemicals to deal with pressure.
			17. Avoiding emotional "overload." (taking on problems of others when you are under stress)
	✓		18. Giving and accepting positive "strokes."
	✓		19. Talking out troubles and getting professional help if needed.
	✓		20. Selecting emotional "investments" more carefully.
✓			21. Taking breaks at work when needed.

30   13 x 3   2
              3   9

SCORE YOURSELF

If your score was between 21 and 50, there are several areas you need to develop to better release your stress. It might be a good idea to discuss some of your answers with a counselor or close friend.

If you scored between 51 and 75, you have discovered a variety of ways to deal effectively with stress. Make a note of those items you checked "need to improve" and work on strategies to help you move to the "I'm Average" box.

If your score was 75 or greater — congratulations. You have found some excellent ways to deal with frustration and the complexities of life.

This exercise was adapted from *Mental Fitness: A Guide to Emotional Health,* by Merrill F. Raber, M.S.W., Ph.D. and George Dyck, M.D. For order information, see the back of this book.

Block #4

Following the Rules

While some rules are obviously necessary (i.e. we should all be happy that there is a consensus agreement about stopping at red lights), others thwart innovation because they encourage a mentally lazy acceptance of the status quo. Many inventions and innovations to a particular industry have been brought about by people outside of that industry. Why? Because the people who make the creative breakthroughs are not hampered by knowing all the rules and limitations.

Blockbuster #4

Breaking the Rules

It is not always a bad idea to break certain rules — especially as they pertain to your daily routine. Which ones of the following "rule breakers" would you like to try? (Mark it with an X and write the date you'll put it in practice.)

RULE BREAKER	DATE
_____ Take a different route to work in the morning.	_____
_____ Eat lunch at new restaurant.	_____
__✓__ Eat a different kind of food at lunch.	_____
__✓__ Skip lunch and go roller-skating or jogging.	_____
_____ Ask for something outlandish.	_____
_____ Come to work in the morning and pretend it is your first day there. Write your reactions.	_____
_____ Come to work in the morning and pretend you were a customer or a competitor. Then write up your reactions.	_____
__✓__ Sign up for an activity you have never tried before.	_____
_____ Invite someone you don't know to have lunch or a conversation with you.	_____
__✓__ Read a book on a topic about which you know nothing.	_____
__✓__ Take a weekend to go somewhere you have never been.	_____
_____ Ask for advice or input from someone whose opinion you have never sought (spouse, child, janitor, client, stranger).	_____
_____ Break the "elevator rules" and stand facing the rear.	_____

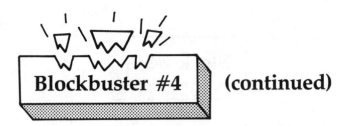

Blockbuster #4 (continued)

What Other Rules Would You Like to Break?　　　　Date

The Rule of "them + us"

Cloting Rule

What is Preventing You from Breaking Them?

I don't like "them"

MORE BLOCKS AND BLOCKBUSTERS AHEAD

Block #5

Making Assumptions

A recent story told about how the Research and Development manager of a large high tech firm found supplies and test equipment missing from a laboratory store, so he ordered the installation of a security system. Several months passed without any further losses.

While preparing a routine report for the President of the firm, the manager noticed that progress on a couple of key projects had slowed down. Concerned, he decided to investigate. He discovered that several technical research engineers had stopped working on the projects at home on weekends because they could no longer get supplies and test equipment. The R & D manager had erroneously assumed the missing supplies were caused by dishonest employees. He had therefore, "solved" the wrong problem. Making iron clad assumptions often inhibits creative thinking about other possibilities.

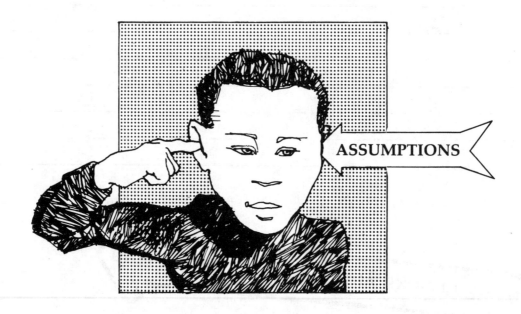

ASSUMPTIONS

Blockbuster #5

Checking Assumptions

To avoid solving the wrong problem while also opening your creative thinking to possible solutions, it is wise to check your assumptions. Begin by asking yourself questions like:

What are the most likely possibilities?

What am I taking for granted?

What are some other possible explanations?

For example, you are at a library and you see a woman put two books in her bag and begin to walk out. What are some possible assumptions?

1. She is stealing the books.

2. She is the librarian.

3. They are her books.

What else?

4. ___She already checked them out___

5. ___She purchased them___

6. _____

What could you do to find out if one of the possible assumptions is accurate? (Write your response in the space provided below).

Ask the lady

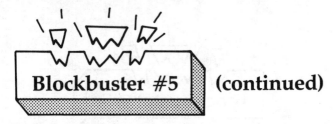

Blockbuster #5 (continued)

Checking Assumptions

Based on each assumption from the exercise on the previous page what would a possible solution be? (Notice that each assumption leads to a different variety of solutions.)

Can you think of anything at work where your assumptions might be leading you to solve the wrong problem?

How can you check for accuracy?

> **It Always Makes Sense to Check
> Your Assumptions!**

Making Assumptions - Puzzle

Nine Dots Puzzle

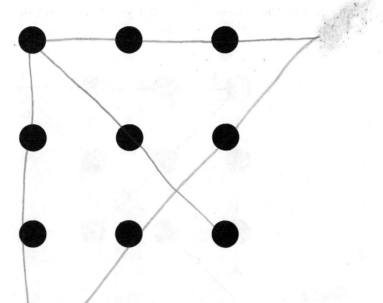

The instructions are to draw four straight lines that go through all nine dots by never taking your pen or pencil off the paper. If you have trouble with this, check your **assumptions** about the **rules.** Can you find the solution? If you are really creative, the nine dots puzzle can be solved with three straight lines. Good luck!

(The solution for the nine dot puzzle is given on the next page.)

Assumptions Puzzle (continued)

Solutions

To solve the puzzle with four straight lines, you must challenge your assumption that the "rules" meant for you to stay within the dots.

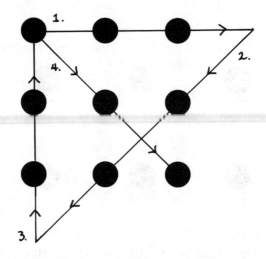

To solve the puzzle with three straight lines, you don't have to go through the center of each dot! (At least the rules do not so specify.)

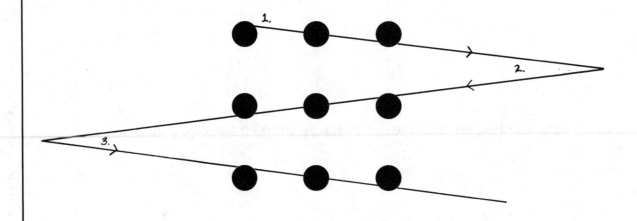

Block #6

Over-Reliance on Logic

Dr. Jonas Salk, developer of the Salk vaccine, said, "When I became a scientist, I would picture myself as a virus or cancer cell and try to imagine what it would be like to be either." Einstein wrote that "Imagination is more powerful than knowledge."

Highly creative thinkers see the advantage of going beyond logical problem-solving techniques to include imagination, intuition, emotion and/or humor.

Blockbuster #6

Your "Internal" Creative Climate

1. Write out one problem you have been trying to solve using a purely logical approach.

2. Staying open-minded and with a positive mental attitude, close your eyes and let your body relax. State the problem clearly to yourself.

3. Turn the situation over to your imagination, your intuition, your feelings and your sense of humor. Play with possibilities, insights, absurdities. Don't judge your thoughts, just let them come.

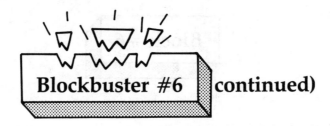

Your Internal Creative Climate (continued)

4. Write out key words or thoughts until you feel yourself "pushing" for additional ideas.

5. Flesh out your ideas by writing for five or ten minutes—allow one thought to lead to another.

6. Retrace your steps to "play with" and discover additional aspects.

Block #7

Believing You Are Not Creative

Ninety percent of the knowledge about the human brain and creativity has been discovered in the past ten years. UCLA's Brain Research Institute research indicates that the creative capacity of the human brain is potentially limitless. The only restrictions are self-imposed through our belief systems.

The largest obstacle you may ever have to face is an absolute acceptance of what you believe is or is not possible for you to accomplish.

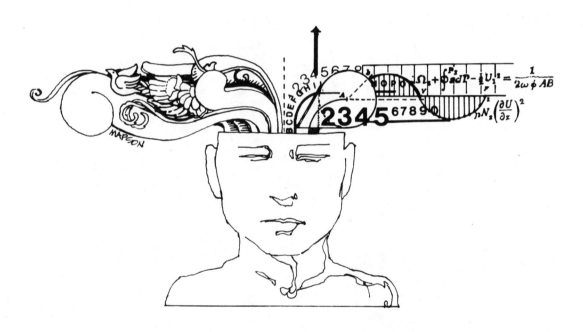

If You Believe You Can or If You Believe You Can't . . . . You're Right

Blockbuster #7

Creative Beliefs

The human brain is often compared to a computer; using this comparison, it is easy to see that creative results require creative programming!

List those beliefs about yourself that would help you grow into a more creative person.

1. Always asking why!!

2.

3.

4.

5.

6.

7.

8.

9.

10.

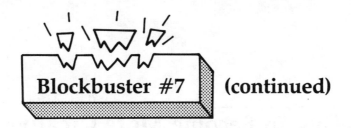

Blockbuster #7 (continued)

Some beliefs stand in the way of your creativity. These are the "garbage" in the acronym GIGO (garbage in, garbage out). List examples of your nonproductive goals here.

1.

2.

3.

4.

5.

6.

7.

8.

9.

10.

When you have completed this list, take a black marker and cross-off each idea on the list. Whenever one of the limiting beliefs you wrote down comes into your thoughts, remember you chose to eliminate it. Replace it with a more productive belief that you have decided to retain.

15 Ways To Become More Creative

Check those you intend to use within the next month. I plan to:

☑ 1. Ask "what if" questions—the crazier the better. (What if we all wore jeans to work? What if we got paid every day? What if my boss had to work for me one day a week?)

☑ 2. Make up metaphors and analogies. A brain is like a bank—you can only take out as much as you put in. My job is like _____

_____

☐ 3. Pay attention to small ideas. That's where many big ones get their start.

☐ 4. Daydream. Let your mind wander.

☐ 5. Play "Just Suppose." (Just suppose I decided to ask for a raise . . . Just suppose I found a better way to serve our customers . . . . . . Just suppose.)

☐ 6. Try different ways of expressing your creativity. (Cooking, painting, photography, writing, playing tennis, inventing, hosting parties, etc.)

☐ 7. Notice when you do do something creative and keep a CREATIVITY SUCCESS file.

☐ 8. Learn and play strategy games like chess, checkers, backgammon, or bridge.

☐ 9. Learn a foreign language (and force your brain to think in new patterns).

☐ 10. If you're right-handed, try using your left hand to do things. If you're left-handed, switch to your right for a while.

☐ 11. Guess at measurements rather than using a yard stick, a tape measure or a cup. Then measure and see how close you were.

☐ 12. Balance your checkbook without using a calculator.

☐ 13. Read three-quarters of a novel, then stop and write your own ending.

☐ 14. Stand on your head to get the blood really flowing to your brain.

☐ 15. Do jigsaw and crossword puzzles.

SECTION III:
TECHNIQUES FOR IDEA GENERATION

What Did You Learn in School?

If you were to go into an average college classroom of seniors and put a large dot on the blackboard, how do you think they'd answer the question, "What is that?"

Would you agree that the most likely answer would be, "A dot!"

Now what if you did the same thing in front of a class of kindergarten children? What kinds of answers do you suppose you'd hear?

Somewhere between the beginning and the end of our formal education, we have developed ways to find the "right" answer, but lost the creative impetus to go beyond the other possible right answers.

What Helps or Hinders?

Linus Pauling, the Nobel prizewinning scientist, said: "The best way to get good ideas is to have lots of ideas." Highly creative thinkers agree that the first step in becoming more innovative is to generate lots of possibilities.

Some habits and behaviors encourage the production of ideas while others stop idea generation completely. Which of these actions are you most likely to do?

HINDERS	HELPS
Do you most often:	or:
_____ look for the *right* answer	_____ look for lots of possible right answers
_____ approach problem solving as "serious" business	_____ have fun with problem solving and "play" with ideas
_____ avoid making mistakes as much as possible	_____ accept mistakes as a natural byproduct of the creative process
_____ push yourself even when tired to keep working on the problem	___✓___ take deliberate breaks when you put the problem on the "back burner"
_____ ask advice only from "experts"	___✓___ get input from a variety of sources
_____ dismiss your "silly" ideas	___✓___ use your sense of humor as a rich source of possibilities
_____ tell your idea only to people who will agree with it or support it	___✓___ encourage feedback from a variety of sources including a "Devil's Advocate"
_____ keep quiet when you don't understand something	___✓___ risk asking "dumb" questions
_____ follow the motto "If it ain't broke, don't fix it"	_____ continually look to improve all products, services and systems
_____ do not have a system to record ideas that come to you	_____ keep an "idea journal" and record all good ideas

The One Minute Idea Generator

In one minute, take a piece of paper and list as many uses for a paperclip as you can think of. Here are some suggestions to keep in mind.

1. Go for quantity, not quality of ideas.
2. Write down *every* idea. Do not judge or criticize!
3. Stay relaxed, playful, even silly.
4. Switch your point of view. (Look at the paperclip as if you were an insect, as if you were lost in the desert, as if you were a designer, etc.)
5. Ask yourself, "What if?" questions. (What if the paperclip were straightened out and a hole drilled through the middle? What if a bunch of them were linked together? What if one end was sharpened to a point?)

Ready now, time yourself for one minute. *Ready — set — go.*

(You may wish to use a separate sheet of paper)

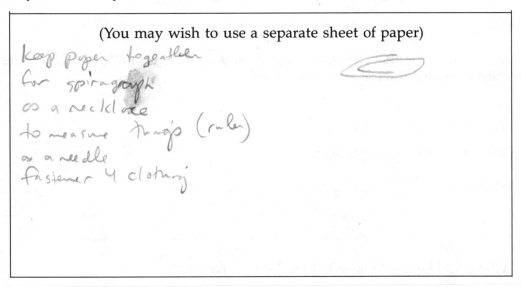

keep paper together
for spiragraph
as a necklace
to measure things (ruler)
as a needle
fastener 4 clothing

How did you do? Were you able to keep writing the full minute? Did you run out of ideas? Or do you still have ideas coming?

(Note to managers/trainers: This exercise, using various common objects, is an excellent "warm-up" technique before a brainstorming session).

Idea-Generating Questions

An excellent technique for generating ideas is the use of Idea-Generating Questions. It can serve as a checklist for possibilities. When you use a checklist such as this, start with a particular item and think about ways to expand it.

1. What else can it be used for? (without any changes)

2. What could be used instead? What else is like this?

3. How could it be adopted or modified for a new use?

4. What if it were larger (thicker, heavier, stronger)?

5. What if it were smaller (thinner, lighter, shorter)?

6. How might it be rearranged? (reversed?)

7. etc.

Example: Imagine that the object you're thinking of is an umbrella. Using the checklist complete the following exercise:

1. What else could it be used for?

   Possible answer — to dig holes.

   What else?   _as a cane_

   picking up garbage

   carrying groceries

2. What could be used instead? What else is like this?

   Possible answer — a newspaper held over your head.

   What else?   _a plastic bag_

   books

   a coat

Idea-Generating Questions (continued)

3. How could it be adapted for a new use?

   Possible answer—add a flashlight to the handle for people who go out on a dark, rainy day.

   What else? _put ropes to make a backpack_
   waterproof to make a boat

4. What if it were larger (thicker, heavier, stronger)?

   Possible answer—make it double size to cover two people.

   What else? _would make a tent_
   sun shade
   awning over house door

5. What if it were smaller (thinner, lighter, shorter)?

   Possible answer—make it small enough to fold up and fit inside a purse.

   What else? _to put over dog house_

6. How might it be rearranged? (reversed)?

   Possible answer—turn it upside down and make a birdbath out of it.

   What else? _____

Different Points of View

Creative thinking begins with idea generation. If you are to have the broadest perspective on a situation, at some point you will need to consider different viewpoints from all people who are involved. The skill of deliberately shifting your point of view to accomodate those of others will allow you to create a more complete list of the factors, consequences and options involved.

For example, if a chemical company is developing a new pesticide to increase crop yields, it would be to their advantage to consider the following points of view:

- **The Farmer:** Interested in cost of product and how it is applied. Encouraged by reports of increased yield. Concerned about possible toxicity to people and animals.

- **The Company:** Wants more information on production costs, the source of the ingredients, the potential market size, and the expected profit margin.

- **The Consumer:** Worried about the effects of the product on health, taste of food and price to be paid in the market.

- **The Environmentalist:** Concerned about pollution, contamination and the ecological effects on the food chain.

- **Others:**   (add your own)

_____

_____

_____

_____

_____

Office Automation Exercise

Assume that you are the manager of a large personnel department and you want to automate by putting your entire office staff on computers. Most have never used computers before. The office manager responsible for managing them has been with the company for twenty years. What do you suppose would be the different points of view when you announce your plan?

— Your Boss:

— Your Office Manager:

— The Office Staff:

— Other Departments in the Organization:

— Are there other points of view you should consider?

Split Brain Theory

In 1981 Roger Sperry was awarded the Nobel Prize for his proof of the split brain theory. According to Dr. Sperry, the brain has two hemispheres with different but overlapping functions. The right and left hemispheres of the brain each specialize in distinct types of thinking processes.

In general, in 95 percent of all right-handed people, the left side of the brain not only cross controls the right side of the body, but is also responsible for analytical, linear, verbal and rational thought. (In most left-handed people, the hemispheric functions are reversed.) It is a left-brain function you rely on when balancing your checkbook, remembering names and dates, or setting goals and objectives. Since most of our concepts of thinking come from Greek logic, left-brained processes are most rewarded in our education system.

The right hemisphere controls the left side of the body and is holistic, imaginative, nonverbal, and artistic. Whenever you recall someone's face, become engrossed in a symphony, or simply daydream, you are engaging in right-brain function. Right-brain processes are less often rewarded in school.

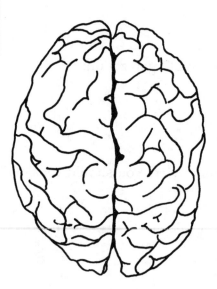

Left Hemisphere	**Right Hemisphere**
Logic	Intuition
Sequential	Nonverbal
Verbal	Visual
Linear	Spacial
Analytical	Creative
Rational	Holistic
Explicit	Artistic
	Humorous/Playful

Whole Brain Problem Solving

Creative problem-solvers understand that both hemispheres of the brain (both thinking processes) are valuable. The trick lies in knowing which function best support a particular phase of the problem-solving process.

Left: Logically define the problem.

Right: Generate creative possibilities and alternative solutions.

Left: Pragmatically evaluate ideas to determine which are applicable.

Left: Prepare a strategic plan for gaining support and implementing the solution.

Right: Persuade others by sharing your vision and commitment.

In the idea generation phase, right brain functions become most helpful. Have you ever struggled to solve a problem and found the answer "popped" into your head while you showered or jogged or upon waking? That is because it was released from left-brain control and turned over to your right-brain insight.

The manager of human resources at a manufacturing company in Pittsburg is most effective generating ideas when she is meditating. The vice president of strategic planning at a San Francisco communications company gets his best ideas during his running. A marketing representative likes to "sleep on it", telling himself he'll have fresh ideas in the morning. A salesperson tells jokes and laughs her way into new insights. None of these people are aware they are shifting brain hemisphere function. All of them simply know (from trial and error) how to get the results they need.

Whole Brain Problem Solving (continued)

Where Do You Get Your Best Ideas?

_____

_____

_____

_____

The Creative Idea Journal

To capture good ideas whenever and wherever they occur, take a pocket-sized notebook and write at the top of page 1 this question: "In what ways might I . . . .?" (fill in with your own problem). Place the notebook in your purse or pocket. Without focusing on it, let your unconscious mind "incubate" the problem and deliver possible solutions as they "pop up" throughout the day. Enter each idea with the time of day it occurred and the activity you were engaged in at the moment. By the end of the week, you will not only have several usable ideas, you will also know more about your creative "schedule."

IDEA JOURNAL
"IN WHAT WAYS MIGHT I . . . ."

Intuition

▶ The president of a large restaurant chain headquartered in Vancouver, British Columbia, flabbergasted his underlings when he made a command decision to build a restaurant in a rundown warehouse area. Two years later the new restaurant was the chain's top moneymaker and the neighborhood around it was revitalized.

▶ The board chairman of a small Australian airline company calls his treasurer frequently and tells him to stand by to spend some money on replacement equipment. Within days, one of the airline's planes unexpectedly needs a costly part.

▶ A plant manager of one of a leading U.S. software company spends most of her time sitting at her desk doing paperwork. But every once in a while she gets up from her desk, and for reasons not clear to her, walks to a point on the production line and picks out a software diskette that appears to be okay but proves to be flawed.

Whether they call it a hunch, a gut feeling, or even ESP, thousands of managers and executives make business deals based on their intuition. Think back over your life. Have you ever had a hunch that you should or should not be doing something? We all have hunches, but many of us ignore or distrust them as being irrational and useless.

Creative thinkers tend to pay more attention to their feelings, including what they call their "inner voice." Management professor Weston Agor studied hundreds of top managers and found a disproportionate percentage used intuition as an important part of their decision-making process. Most managers first digested all the relevant information and data available, but when the data was conflicting or incomplete, they relied on intuitive approaches to come to a conclusion.

How Intuitive Are You?

Answer the next ten questions by indicating your agreement or disagreement with each statement.

1. I believe in ESP (extra sensory perception). (YES) NO

2. I have had occasions where I knew exactly what was going to happen beforehand. (YES) NO

3. I trust my instincts when I meet someone for the first time. (YES) NO

4. I often have flashes of insight about an important project. YES (NO)

5. Many of my best decisions were made by "going with my gut feeling." (YES) NO

6. I can often sense a problem before anyone tells me there is one. YES NO

7. I have days when I do well just because I feel especially lucky. YES NO

8. I have had what others would call a psychic experience. (YES) NO

9. Sometimes I am able to dream the answer to a problem. (YES) NO

10. If all the data supported one opinion and my intuition led me strongly to a conflicting decision, I would follow my intuition. YES NO

YES scores of 5 or more indicate a high reliance on intuition. NO scores of 5 or more show a low reliance on intuition.

How Intuitive Are You? (continued)

Ways to Increase Your Business Intuition

1. *Practice Foretelling the Future.* If you are going to have a business meeting with people you haven't met yet, guess as to how they'll look, what they'll wear and how they will approach the business they plan to conduct. If you're looking for a parking space, anticipate where the first open space will be.

2. *Imagine Yourself Doing a Task Before the Fact.* Not only will you prime your brain for actually doing the task, you will be able to compare your actual performance to the image in your mind.

3. *Notice Feelings and Inner Sensations You Usually Ignore.* Pay attention to internal stirring and feelings. By monitoring them constantly, you are more likely to catch those changes that indicate something has registered unconsciously.

4. *Keep An Idea Journal.* Write down flashes of insight and keep a record of decisions you made on this basis. As you reflect on this "diary" later, you'll be able to evaluate your accuracy.

5. *Meditate or Learn Self-Hypnosis.* Insights are most likely to occur when you first quiet the conscious mind's chatter, then concentrate (focus your attention on one thing) and become receptive to creative ideas bubbling up through the subconscious.

6. *Visualize Symbolically.* When faced with a problem person or situation, create a mental picture that is symbolically representative. (For example, a nurse visualized her confrontations with the hospital's administration as Don Quixote tilting at windmills.) Notice any new, creative ideas that come to you as a result of looking at your situation in a unique way.

Creative Imagination

This exercise requires at least two people; one to guide the process and one or more others to participate.

- **Step 1:** The participant(s) begin by choosing a specific problem or issue for which he/she/they would like additional insights and possibilities.

- **Step 2:** The guide reads the following script slowly:

Script*

Guide: "Find a comfortable position, either sitting or lying down. Close your eyes and focus your attention on your breathing. Inhale deeply. *(Pause)* Exhale fully. *(Repeat several times)* With each exhalation think the word RELAX. Allow yourself to begin releasing any physical tension you feel as you imagine a flow of relaxation throughout your body, from the top of your head to the tips of your toes. *(Pause for a few seconds)* Let yourself relax deeply .... comfortably....... completely. Now as I count from 10 to 1, imagine yourself riding in an elevator....... a very special elevator.......going deeper with every number I count. *(Count slowly)* 10 - 9 - 8 - 7 -6 - 5 - 4 - 3 - 2 - 1. As you get off the elevator, you enter a very special room. It is your CREATIVITY ROOM, decorated just the way you like it........ with furniture, colors, wall decorations and equipment of your choice. You feel instantly safe and at home here. *(Pause for a few seconds).*

In a moment you will hear a knock on the door announcing the arrival of your CREATIVITY CONSULTANT. This may be someone you know and have consciously chosen to assist you. Or, your counselor may have been selected subconsciously, and you will be surprised when that person appears. In any event, your counselor is symbolic of your creative potential. *(Pause).* Now hear the knock and go to the door to greet your consultant. *(Pause)* Open the door. *(Pause)*

---

*The audio cassette tape of *Creative Imagination* (this exercise recorded by Carol Kinsey Goman) is available from Kinsey Consulting Services, P.O. Box 8255, Berkeley, California, 94707. (415) 943-7850.

Creative Imagination Exercise (continued)

Invite your consultant into the room and explain your problem situation in full detail. *(Pause)* Ask your consultant for any advice or insight. *(Pause)* Pay attention if your consultant speaks to you. Be receptive to any idea or feeling that occurs. Notice whatever happens. *(Pause)* Ask your consultant for a single word that can help you solve your problem. Listen carefully. *(Pause)* If you hear nothing, just clear your mind and let the first word you think of become your clue. Don't be concerned if there is no obvious connection between this word and your problem. Just accept whatever comes to you as having some hidden value. *(Pause)*

Now thank your consultant and say good-bye. Look around your room one last time. (Pause) Think about the word clue that was given to you as you leave your room and enter the elevator. As I count from 1 to 10, feel yourself coming back to this present time and place. (Count slowly) 1 - 2 - 3 - 4 - 5 - 6 - 7 - 8 - 9 - 10. Open your eyes and say your clue word.

- **Step 3:** Write your word on a blank sheet of paper. Immediately write whatever thoughts come to you. Relate this word to your problem situation. Use free association and write nonstop for at least five minutes.

Phases of Creativity

▶ Phase One   **Preparation:** Laying the groundwork. Gathering research, background information, specific data, various opinions.

▶ Phase Two   **Concentration:** Becoming totally absorbed in the problem or situation.

▶ Phase Three   **Incubation:** Taking time out, a rest period where the total process is turned over to the subconscious mind. Seeking distractions.

▶ Phase Four   **Illumination:** The AHA! experience where insights, possibilities and answers come. Getting that great idea!

▶ Phase Five   **Evaluation:** Testing your ideas by taking them through a checklist of criteria for practical application. Getting feedback, checking assumptions through a pilot project, modifying and improving, gathering support.

▶ Phase Six   **Application:** Innovatively applying the solution. Confronting and solving the problem by using your creativity.

Phases Two, Three and Four

Metaphorical Thinking

Many creative thinkers naturally gravitate to the use of metaphors and analogies in their everyday speech and thought patterns. As a result, their perceptions of situations are normally more colorful and original.

Long accepted as a potent tool for the creative worker, Aristotle wrote that "the greatest thing by far, is to be the master of metaphor." He regarded metaphoric ability (which implies the discernment of linkages between disimilar objects and conditions) as a mark of genius.

Rules, regulations, and conventions give us order and security. With them we tend to shy away from that which is unknown, strange or different. One way to expand our creative problem-solving is to bypass convention and gain insights through comparison.

1. List as many answers as you can to the question:

How is an iceberg like a good idea?

Examples:

— You may have to go a long way to find one.

— Most of it doesn't show.

What else?

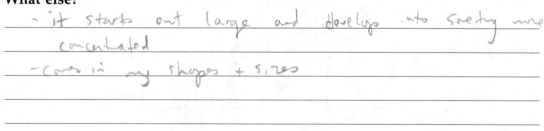

- it starts out large and develops into something more concentrated
- comes in many shapes + sizes

Metaphorical Thinking (continued)

2. Now do the same thing with:

How is your job like driving a car on the freeway?

Examples:

— It's a lot easier if everyone follows procedures.

— If you do it in the afternoon, it's hard to stay awake.

What else?

- there are a lot of distractions
- have to share the space with others going the same direction
- trying to get somewhere - end result

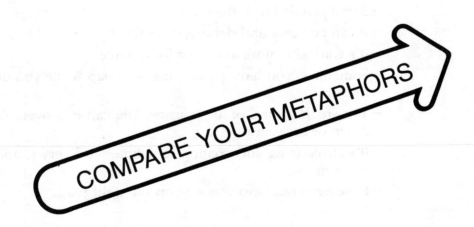

COMPARE YOUR METAPHORS

Metaphorical Thinking (continued)

Author Responses - Metaphorical Thinking

1. How Is An Iceberg Like a Good Idea?

- It floats and moves.
- It is slippery.
- It grows bigger and gets anchored at the bottom.
- You'll know it when you see it.
- It has a commanding presence.
- It gets a chilly reception.
- It doesn't show the work that's gone into it.
- It is 90% submerged and to appreciate its magnitude, you have to look below the surface.
- It sometimes melts away.
- It can be moved to other places.
- It's difficult to come by.
- It's a wonder of nature.
- When conditions are right, many will be created.

2. How Is Your Job Like Driving a Car on the Freeway?

- It's hard to do if you don't keep your eyes open.
- You have to cooperate with other people.
- Some people go faster than others.
- Some people break the rules.
- It can be noisy and dangerous at times.
- It's confusing until you do it for a while.
- Sometimes you have passengers who nap while you do the work.
- You are in control of the journey. You can pull over, slow down or accelerate.
- It's challenging and exciting sometimes and very routine at other times.
- Roadsigns can help you stay on the right road.

Analogy

In science, technology, business, or problem-solving in general, it is frequently a metaphor that provides the key to a new invention or theory. Analogies take metaphoric thinking to the next level by creating a comparison between one event or item and something else that has similar elements.

> **Example:** Life *is like* a grapefruit *in that (or because)* you just start to enjoy it and it squirts you in the eye.
>
> Life *is like* reading a good mystery novel *in that (or because)* the deeper you get into it, the more you wonder how it will turn out.

While creating analogies and using metaphoric thinking, let your imagination and sense of humor go wild. Have fun! Now it's your turn.

Life is like _ice cream_ in that or because _it just seems to melt away_

Life is like _an encyclopedia_ in that or because _there is never an end of things to learn_

Life is like _lottery ticket_ in that or because _you can't always win_

Life is like _____ in that or because _____

Life is like _____ in that or because _____

Problem-Solving Analogies

A classic example of using an analogy to solve problems is one of a defense contractor that developed a missile that had to fit so closely within its silo it couldn't be pushed in. Using the analogy of a horse that refuses to be pushed into a stall, the solution was to lead it in. The solution for the missile company: PULL IT IN WITH A CABLE.

Let's take a look at that process:

Step One: State Problem *(What is the situation?)*

Missile fits so closely within silo that it can't be pushed in. How then to get it in?

Step Two: Create Analogies *(What else **is like** this situation?)*
Generate as many possibilities as you can, then choose one to work with:

Trying to get a horse into its stall.
Trying to get toothpaste back into the tube.
Trying to get a fat lady into her girdle.
Trying to get an item back into its shrink-wrap covering.
Trying to get a car into a too small garage.

Step Three: Solve the Analogy

To get a horse that can't be pushed into its stall you need to lead it in.

Step Four: Transfer Solution to Problem

Lead the missile into the silo by pulling it in with a cable.

YOU CAN DO IT!

PROBLEM

Problem-Solving Analogies (continued)

Here's a Hypothetical Problem for You to Practice Problem Solving with Analogy:

Assume that you are the manager of a large department store. Recently you have been plagued by increasing losses due to shoplifting. How might you reduce shoplifting in your store?

Step One: State Problem *(What is the situation?)* ↑ losses due to shoplifty. How to reduce?

Step Two: Create Analogies

1.

2.

3.

4.

5.

Choose your favorite to work with.

Step Three: Solve the Analogy

Step Four: Transfer Solution to Problem

A possible solution to this problem is outlined on the next page.

Problem Solving Analogies (continued)

Author's Possible Solution Using Analogies

Step One: *State Problem*

How do you keep people from shoplifting?

Step Two: *Create Analogies*
Trying to keep people from shoplifting *is like*:

1. Trying to keep a cat from eating out of an open can of tuna.
2. Trying to keep kids from sneaking cookies out of the cookie jar.
3. Trying to prevent people from jaywalking.
4. Trying to keep bees away from colorful flowers.

Step Three: *Solve the Analogy*

Depending on the analogy chosen, a different list of alternatives will become available

1. How to keep cats from eating out of an open tuna can:

   - cover the can
   - put cat in another room
   - put a dog in the same room
   - put tuna in the refrigerator

2. How to keep kids from sneaking cookies from the cookie jar:

   - hide the jar
   - put a lock on the jar
   - give them cookies

3. How to keep students from cheating:

   - isolate them and monitor them closely
   - penalize them when they're caught
   - give oral exams
   - replace tests with projects

Problem Solving Analogies (continued)

4. How to prevent people from jaywalking:
   - erect barriers along the street
   - increase police presence and issue lots of tickets
   - increase education efforts

5. How to keep bees away from colorful flowers:
   - raise the flowers in a hothouse
   - move the beehive
   - give the bees another source of nectar

Step Four: *Transfer Solution to Problem*

Here are some of the solutions suggested by different analogies:

How to keep people from shoplifting:

- affix electronic anti-theft tags on merchandise that can only be removed by sales staff
- cover the display merchandise with clear plastic
- put customers in special viewing room
- keep merchandise in case
- keep all merchandise but a sample in back room
- give away merchandise (as a reward for catching a shoplifter?)
- have prominently placed video cameras
- prosecute all shoplifters
- treat shoplifting as an illness
- offer support groups and lectures from reformed shoplifters
- develop psychological profile of shoplifters for staff of store
- convert store to catalog sales
- move the store to another area

Problem Solving Analogies (continued)

What is one personal situation where you'd like to try using analogies to solve a problem?

Step One: State Problem

How to stay interested at work?

Trying to keep motivated is like

Step Two: Create Analogies (Your situation is like _____)

1. Trying to wake up a sleepy person

2. A speeder saving $

3.

4.

5.

Step Three: Solve the Analogy

Step Four: Transfer Solution to Problem

Personal Analogies

To work with personal analogies, you must creatively project yourself into the situation and identify with a person or thing to the extent that you imagine how it would feel to be this person or object. In this exercise there are no right or wrong answers—just your personal insights.

For example, in the case of the shoplifting problem, you might choose to identify with the shoplifter. If so, you'd begin by asking yourself questions and answering *as if* you were the thief:

1. *As the shoplifter, what are my thoughts as I walk into the store?, What do I see, hear, touch, taste, or smell in the shoplifting situation?*

   (Begin with the words, "As the shoplifter I am motivated to steal something by . . . . ." and then continue writing using the first person. Let your creative imagination take over.)

   - color
   - if I want it.
   - if everyone else has 1 and I can't afford it
   - getting a thrill out of it
   - trying to get even with the store for something

Personal Analogies Exercise (continued)

2. What are your emotions at the moment of taking something?

- thrill
- fear
- excitement

3. What different types of noises, lights or voices might deter you?

- footsteps closing in
- salesclerk raising her voice
- small child nearby

4. What could happen to cause you to change your mind and not take or return the goods?

- feelings of remorse
- a friend getting caught

Personal Analogy Exercise (Review)

Go back over the pages you have written and look for insights that could lead to possible solutions. By using your imagination in this creative way, you can also personify objects — relating *as if* you were the bridge being built or the project being planned.

List at least five current situations where you could gain insight by using the personal analogy: (There are no right or wrong answers.)

1.

2.

3.

4.

5.

Visual Thinking

Visual aids, in various forms, can be used to boost creativity. Try pinning relevant pictures, notes or cartoons on a wall you regularly see. The resulting "trigger effect" will help your mind incubate ideas and shape solutions.

One interesting form of visual thinking is called "mind mapping." It is simple to do. To begin take a central theme and write or draw it in the center of a sheet of paper. Circle the main theme and draw lines like spokes whenever new ideas come to mind—writing each idea just above the line that is drawn. If one particular idea suggests another association, draw a branch off that line and write in.

For instance, if you were the owner of a health spa and were looking for ways to develop your business, your mind map might look like this:

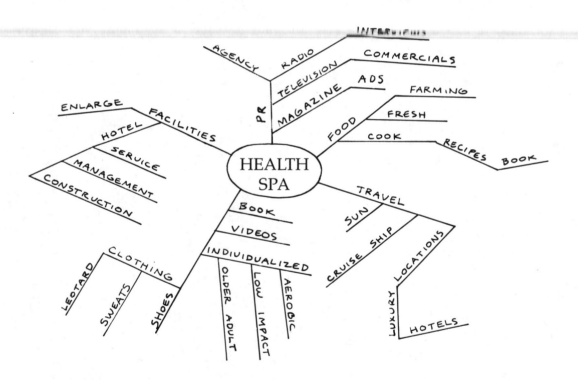

Once you have the knack of letting your mind flow into this visual map, you can use the technique for either business or personal goals. Several corporate executives use mind-mapping to prepare informal talks where there has not been time for preparation. One manager used a mind-map to decide on the structure and purpose of a project team. As author, I use mind maps to chart my annual business goals—and post the map where I'll encounter it daily.

Create Your Own Mind Map

Use the space below to experiment with you own mind map. Think about a complex problem in your life and draw a mind map in the space provided below. (Be inventive. Use small drawings or illustrations. Make your spokes different colors.)

Interviews

Resumé

Finding a New Job

Researching Business

SECTION IV:
GROUP CREATIVITY

Managing For Creativity

Are individuals more creative when working separately or as part of a group? What has your experience been? Of course it will often depend on the personalities involved, but many times we hear of the superior creative efforts of a dedicated group. The product development team of the innovative Macintosh computer at APPLE Computer Corporation was one such example. Why then do so many team efforts fall short of the mark? And what can you as a manager or supervisor do to increase the creative output of your work groups?

Build a Climate for Creativity

A manager must be sensitive to the creative needs of employees and design ways to meet these needs while still achieving the goals of the organization. When the following elements are combined, both individual and corporate success is possible. Check your proficiency below.

I am proficient at:	Do Well	Needs Improving
1. Getting to know employees as individuals to learn their creativity needs.	_____	_____
2. Providing training in the basics of creativity to everyone.	_____	_____
3. Guiding and encouraging personal creativity and growth for all.	_____	_____
4. Recognizing and rewarding creative contribution.	_____	_____
5. Insuring employees realize that you want and expect creative ideas from everyone.	_____	_____
6. Tolerating failure as an expected part of creativity. Making it safe to take risks.	_____	_____
7. Reducing the stress level through understanding, empathy, and humor.	_____	_____
8. Communicating the mission or vision of the organization and showing how each function supports it.	_____	_____
9. Presenting problem situations as challenging opportunities.	_____	_____
10. Inviting creative participation from all those who will be affected by the decision.	_____	_____

Managers who want innovation and creative involvement know how to build a creative climate. If you need to improve — DO IT NOW!

This exercise was adapted from *Team Building,* by Robert Maddux. For order information, use the list in the back of this book.

Creativity in Business

Idea Killers

In order to develop creativity in any group, try to eliminate the following responses to a new idea:

- We tried it before.
- It would take too much time.
- It would cost too much.
- That's not my job.
- That's not your job.
- That's not how we do it here.
- Why don't you put that in writing.
- It's impossible.
- Maybe next year.
- You may be right, but . . . .
- That's a stupid idea.
- Our customer would never go for that.
- You can't do that here.
- My mind is definitely made up.
- I don't think that's important.
- Those people don't count.
- I don't need any more information.
- It's good enough.
- If it ain't broke, don't fix it.
- Our company is too small.
- Our company is too big.
- We don't have time right now.
- That sounds crazy to me.

Add your own.

- we will discuss that at a later date
- Bring that up with your supervisor
-

Idea Growers

Idea growers are those individuals who elicit contributions by presenting problems as open-ended opportunities for input. They will often say:

- Are there any questions?
- Before we make a final decision, let's review all the options.
- Where else can we go for additional information on that?
- In light of the new information, I've changed my mind.
- May I ask a question?
- Excuse me, I don't think I really understood that.
- Is this what you meant?
- I'd like to get your help with an idea I'm working on.
- How could we improve . . . . ?
- What have we missed?
- Who else would be affected?
- What would happen if . . . . ?
- Who else has a suggestion?
- Why do we always do it like that?
- Wouldn't it be fun if . . . . ?
- I don't know much about that. How about you?
- Let me ask you for some ideas on . . . .
- How many ways could we . . . .?
- What ideas have you come up?
- Thank you!

Add your own.

-
-
-

The P - P - C Technique

As a manager who wants to increase the creativity of subordinates, the most important question to ask yourself is: "How do I treat new ideas?" Your management skills may be top notch. In fact, you may even convince everyone that your really want and expect creative contributions. But unless your actions back up your words, you will get nowhere.

It is easy to respond positively to a suggestion or innovation with which you agree. But how do you handle that same enthusiastic contributor who comes up with an idea with which you disagree? Have you ever evaluated the idea so harshly that the person (and anyone else within earshot) is totally demoralized? There is no quicker way to halt creativity from the entire group! On the other hand, you can't accept or endorse every piece of creative input just to protect people's feelings.

Following is a technique that might help. It is called the P-P-C. The P-P-C will provide beneficial feedback in situations where you may have reservations about the proposed idea. The first *P* stands for *POSITIVE*. The first thing you do is comment favorably on things you like about the idea. The second *P* is for *POSSIBILITIES*. This is where you itemize possible applications or extensions of the idea. The *C* represents your *CONCERNS* with the proposal. You express these in a way that says in a straight forward manner, "Here are some concerns I have. Could you help me understand how they could be overcome?" By directing the situation back to the person involved, you allow them to develop a response to your concerns by designing a pilot project, building a model, bringing in other examples of similar situations where there has been success, etc. You also allow them to reconsider and withdraw the idea.

It's best not to judge other's innovations too critically. An irate banker once told Thomas Edison to "get that toy out of my office!", so Edison took his invention (the phonograph) somewhere else.

CASE STUDY →

Case Study #2

Karen is manager of the women's wear section in a major department store. She has been wanting to improve the customer service and has asked for creative suggestions from her sales group. One of them, Judith, proposed the following: "I think we should clear a spot to put in comfortable chairs and a coffee table with newspapers and magazines. Then the husbands and boyfriends of our customers could wait while their partners try on clothes. It would be even nice to serve coffee and maybe even wine."

Karen has some reservations about the suggestion. If she wanted to use the P - P - C as her evaluation, what might her comments be?

Positives (i.e. I like your concern regarding spouses.)

1. I think that is a great idea
2. If the spouse is happy, the customer can relax + try on
3. cloths
4.
5.

Possibilities (i.e. We could have merchandise catalogues for them
             to read while they wait.)

1. Include some toys for children
2.
3.
4.
5.

Concerns (i.e. I don't know if we can dismantle our display area
           to get the needed extra room. How do you think it could
           be handled?)

1. Coffee or wine would be costly and we might have spips on the merchandize
2.
3.
4.
5.

(Remember to state these as "I have this concern. How could <u>you</u> alleviate this for me?")

The P - P - C Technique (continued)

Notes to Yourself

In which situations at work do you want to remember to use the
P - P - C technique?

1.

2.

3.

4.

5.

Take one of these cases and do a sample **P - P - C** right now.

Positives   *Potentials*   *Concerns*

Brainstorming

The most popular group creativity technique is **_Brainstorming_**. Although it is widely practiced, only seldom is it utilized correctly for optimum benefit. Even if you currently use brainstorming, review these rules to check your technique.

Preparation: Prior to the meeting, give each participant an overview of the subject to be brainstormed: the problem statement, background information, etc.

Send each participant a set of brainstorming rules.

Brainstorming Rules: The ideal group size is between 5 and 12 people. Ideally all are familiar with the procedure. A facilitator will lead the group, a recorder will write a record of the ideas expressed (usually on a chalk board or flip chart for the participants to see and review). A timer will also help keep the group moving. The entire group should participate in the idea-generating process.

Part One

Before working on the "real" situation, it is a good idea to begin with a warm-up exercise (preferably something imaginative or silly to relax and loosen-up the group). When you are ready to "set to work", the facilitator should state the problem or situation and invite input.

He or she should:

1. Keep the atmosphere relaxed, fun and free-wheeling.

2. Encourage everyone to participate either with original ideas, or "piggybacking" (adding on to) other people's input.

3. Focus initially on quantity, not quality of ideas. Some groups set a numerical goal (i.e. 25 or 50 ideas) and try to reach it in the alloted time.

4. Urge participants to say anything that occurs to them, no matter how wild or "far out" those ideas may seen.

Brainstorming (continued)

5. Allow appropriate time (20 to 30 minutes) for the idea generation phase. If the group has been too conservative during this part of the session, the facilitator may use an additional 5 minutes and ask, "What are the wildest, most outrageous ideas we can come up with?" (Remember, you may find a gem of an idea that could be altered to fit reality!)

6. During the idea generation phase, no one should be allowed to judge, criticize or squelch any of the ideas generated. The facilitator should stay alert for nonproductive comments such as, "We tried that last year," "That would cost too much," "I don't think that will work," etc. and counter with, "This isn't the time for evaluation yet."

Break: Before you begin part two of brainstorming, the group should be thanked for their participation to the idea generation phase. Then the team needs to put closure to part one and take a break before going on. (Indeed, one creative twist that can be effective is to use two groups for generating ideas and switch lists of possibilities for evaluation.)

Part Two

The group should reassemble to evaluate the input. As this happens, be sure that each member is familiar with the criteria essential for the evaluation. For instance, if price, human resources, or timing is important, let everyone know. Look at all ideas and suggestions for the value they might contain both as originally stated and altered slightly. See if you can scale down an outrageous idea to one which has practical dimensions.

Follow Up: Regardless of the results of the session, all team members should be thanked for participating. (A short note may be appropriate.) If ideas were suggested that management decides not to implement, your feedback to the group should be in the form of a P - P - C response. If a solution that came from the session is accepted, the entire group must receive full credit!

Brainwriting

With some groups, especially where there is a reluctance to contribute ideas verbally, another technique called *Brainwriting* can replace the more traditional brainstorming. With brainwriting, you follow a similar set of rules, but instead of speaking the ideas, participants will write them.

Preparation: Prior to the meeting, give each participant an overview of the subject to be brainwritten: the problem statement, background information, etc.

Send each participant a set of brainwriting rules.

Brainwriting Rules: This can be used with a group of almost any size, broken down into subgroups of 4–6. Each group should be seated around a small table. Provide each member of the group with a sheet of paper divided into four columns. A facilitator then explains the rules and announces the amount of time alloted to the session (usually 20–30 minutes).

Part One

1. At the top of each participants paper should be a brief description of the problem or situation.

2. Participants are instructed to write four ideas or comments—one in each column.

3. Once a person has completed the four items, he or she puts the paper face down in the center of the table. When all are completed, someone should shuffle the papers and each party takes one that was written by another participant.

4. At this point everyone will have a piece of paper with four items filled in by another person in the group. On this paper the participants write four more items, either additional original ideas or ideas "piggybacked" on those on the page. This paper is then returned face down to the center of the table.

5. This process is continued until the participants run out of things to write, no matter how wild or "far out" those ideas may seem.

Brainwriting (continued)

Break: Before beginning part two of brainwriting, the group(s) should be thanked for their participation in the idea generation phase.

Part Two

Before the group reassembles to evaluate the input, a recorder should collect and compile lists of the input. Make sure that each member is familiar with the criteria essential for the evaluation. Look at all ideas and suggestions for the value they might contain both as originally stated and altered slightly. See if you can scale down an outrageous idea to practical dimensions.

Follow Up: Just as with Brainstorming, team members should be recognized and thanked, suggestions not accepted should be addressed, and suggestions accepted should be credited to the group.

Forced Connections

Many products have been developed by forcing a connection between two seemingly unrelated things: some examples include the clock-radio, the wrist watch and the car stereo to name a few. When participants of a group idea generating session begin to run out of ideas, a facilitator can ask them to look around the room, take something from the environment, and force a connection.

Example

Imagine you are part of a product development team looking at ways to improve the common bathtub. What are some improvements your group might come up with?

1. Make it bigger.
2. Route the warm water to go through pipes to heat the towel rack.
3. Attach a snack tray for those who like to eat in the tub.

What else?

4. Put a seat so you don't slip around

5. Have it insulated to hold the heat

6. Make it longer

7. Put a head Rest and Magazine Rack on

8.

9.

10

Forced Connections (continued)

Your group runs out of things to say and the facilitator should ask participants to look around the room and select three objects. (*Do so where you are now.*) What are they? *Lights, ball, blanket*

What ideas might you get for improving a bathtub from each of these things? (A clock might suggest a timer for the tub, a notepad could bring to mind some sort of waterproof tablet and marker, a chair could suggest an entirely different shape, etc.)

Illuminate the tub
Put special massage balls on the bottom 4 your feet

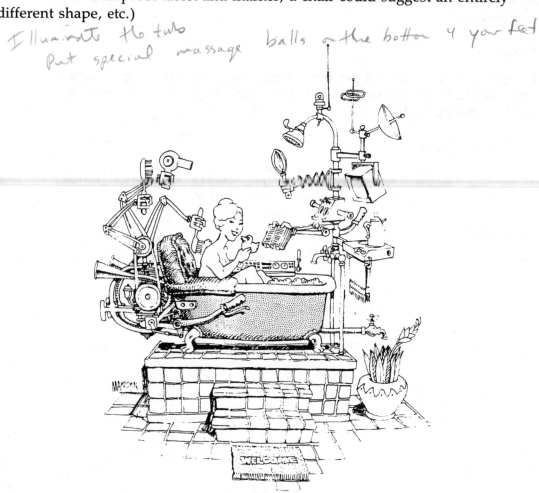

The "Get Fired" Technique

A favorite way to end a group problem-solving session is to ask participants to take the last few minutes and contribute ideas that would probably work, but are so outrageous they could get the group fired. (Obviously, the task then becomes the scaling or toning down the solution so that the problem is solved without risking any jobs!)

SECTION V: INNOVATION AND PRACTICAL SOLUTIONS

The Politics of Creativity

You may have the best creative idea in the history of your organization. Unless, however, you know how to persuade others to support and finance your idea it may never come to light. The "politics" of creativity require a strategic plan to gather information, convince key people, build coalitions and obtain trusted feedback.

Selling Your Creative Ideas

To turn your creative idea into an innovative reality, you must be able to gather the support of key people in your organization. The following test measures how well you are prepared to sell your idea to the decision-makers.

Answer *T* if the statement is mostly true and *F* if mostly false:

1. Being power conscious in your organization is unworthy of your creative efforts. ___F___ ✓

2. It is impossible to figure out what will motivate someone else to support your ideas. ___F___ ✓

3. The only people you will have to sell your ideas to are your superiors. ___F___ ✓

4. It is generally a good plan to "run your idea" by people in advance of asking for their support. ___T___ ✓

5. One way to gather support for your project is to ask for input from those you expect will be most affected. ___T___ ✓

6. A good idea is often defeated by irrelevant issues. ___T___ ✓

7. Unless people are willing to give you total support, it is best to withdraw your request for their help. ___F___ ✓

8. It is wise to get more support, resources, capital, etc. than you think you'll need. ___T___ ✓

Selling Your Creative Ideas (continued)

9. People who "invest" in your idea will hope to get something in return.   _T_

10. It is better to persuade people, even if you have the power to order them to support your idea.   _T_

11. It is important to convert all of your opponents to support your idea.   _F_ ✓

12. It is counterproductive to ask for feedback before your idea has been thoroughly thought out.   _F_ ✓

13. You should be sure to get total credit for any innovative ideas you create.   _X F_

14. When selling an idea, any time is as good as any other.   _F_ ✓

15. People are mostly convinced to back new ideas based on the logical details of a presentation.   _X F_

16. The appraisal of your new idea will probably have nothing to do with power and company politics.   _F_

17. The more you know about the people to whom you are selling your idea, the better you can tailor your presentation.   _T_ ✓

18. It is important for you to support other people's good ideas.   _T_ ✓

19. Unless your idea generates a major change, you should expect little or no resistance.   _F_

20. If you really believe in your idea, you should never alter or "compromise" it.   _F_ ✓

(Answers on Next Page)

Answers to "Selling Your Creative Ideas"

1. False. Being aware that the power structure of your organization is imperative to your getting your creative efforts recognized.
2. False. While it may be difficult, the more you research and can address the needs/concerns of your "audience", the better your chances of success.
3. False. It may be essential to ultimately sell your ideas to key executives. But many people at different levels in your organization have the power to help or hinder your efforts.
4. True.
5. True.
6. True.
7. False. Many people may only be willing (or able) to give limited or conditional support to your project. These supporters can still be useful.
8. True.
9. True.
10. True.
11. False. You will probably never be able to convert every person who opposes your idea.
12. False. It can be an opportunity to iron-out flaws early if you get advance feedback from those whose opinions you trust.
13. False. A manager once said: "It is amazing what can be accomplished as long as I don't insist on sole credit for the innovation."
14. False. Timing the presentation and the selling of your idea is a crucial part of your strategic plan for success.
15. False. While a solid, logical presentation is important, more people are impressed by the depth of your conviction and enthusiasm.
16. False. It is just as realistic to state that the appraisal of your new idea will have *everything* to do with power and company politics.
17. True.
18. True.
19. False. Resistance to new ideas should always be anticipated if there is any change.
20. False. Most good ideas have been altered to better fit a particular climate or application.

Interpretation

Give yourself two points for every correct answer and zero if it was wrong. Your score represents your overall understanding of what it takes to sell your idea.

Low Level		Medium Level	High Level	
0	10	20	30	40

36

Strengthening Your Presentation

When presenting your new idea, you may bolster your position by citing an outside source. See if you can strengthen your argument by including:

— examples from other organizations (within or outside of your field) who have used a similar idea successfully. If others are doing something similar and it works, your organization may feel safer in trying it.

— business and technical journals which have published articles on ideas similar to yours. Quoting from relevant published materials can add credence to your statements.

— consultants who have experience implementing new ideas in other organizations. Not only can they help you plan your strategy, they may also be quoted on their unique perspectives on the implementation process of others.

— company publications in which articles appear on the topic of change, creativity or innovative contributions. If you can use direct statements from top executives that support your position (and then hand out a reproduction of the article quoted) you may gain strength.

— recent organizational data including charts, graphs, etc. which deal directly with your topic and its cost/added value to the organization. Looking prepared and informed will build your creativity.

Basic Consideration in Selling an Idea

Success in launching a new idea or program depends to a large degree on how well you have strategized the "selling" of your idea. The political aspects of your plan require a sensitivity to the power structure in your organization, especially on knowing how your idea addresses the wants or needs of others.

Here are some basic items to consider when developing your strategic plan: Ask yourself these questions early and often!

What are my personal assets and strengths? _____

_____

_____

_____

_____

What are my personal weaknesses and liabilities? _____

_____

_____

_____

_____

Who will be affected if my idea gets implemented? _____

_____

_____

_____

_____

Who are (or can become) my major allies? _____

_____

_____

_____

_____

Who will be my opponents? _____

_____

_____

_____

Basic Considerations in Selling an Idea (continued)

Why will supporters back me? (How will their interest or concerns be addressed?)_____

_____

_____

What are the strengths and weaknesses of my opponents? _____

_____

_____

_____

Where can I anticipate resistance and how can I minimize its impact? _____

_____

_____

_____

Who will I need to add to my coalition of supporters? _____

_____

_____

_____

_____

How can I attract these individuals? _____

_____

_____

_____

_____

Who can I count on for feedback I can trust? _____

_____

_____

_____

Basic Considerations in Selling an Idea (continued)

How will the implementation of my idea serve the mission of the organization?

_____
_____
_____
_____
_____

What is the competition doing in this area? _____

_____
_____
_____

How much of my idea am I willing to alter? _____

_____
_____
_____
_____

How could I implement or test this idea in a way that would minimize the risk for myself and others? _____

_____
_____
_____
_____

Why am I so committed to this idea? _____

_____
_____
_____
_____

My Personal Assessment and Action Plan

The best intentions in the world lead nowhere unless they are put into action. You already have all the creative potential you will ever need. Now it's up to you to apply that creativity in your daily work. By completing this book you are well on your way to increasing your creativity and innovation on the job. You have learned many creative techniques. Where will you use them?

Current Applications of Creativity for Business (Where in your work life do you already express your creativity?)

With discussions with customers

Areas in Business Where You Could Use More Creativity (Where do you feel a need for more creativity and innovation?)

With management and politics in the office

Creativity Resources (What specific techniques from the book could you use to increase your creativity where it's needed?)

Action Plan (continued)

(When specifically are you going to put these creativity techniques into action?)

Situation   **Date**

1. _____

Creativity Technique

_____

Situation   **Date**

2. _____

Creativity Technique

_____

Situation   **Date**

3. _____

Creativity Technique

_____

Situation   **Date**

4. _____

Creativity Technique

_____

Situation   **Date**

5. _____

Creativity Technique

_____

NOTES

NOTES

NOTES

NOTES

NOTES

NOTES

CRISP WORLDWIDE DISTRIBUTION

English language books are distributed worldwide. Major international distributors include:

ASIA/PACIFIC

Australia/New Zealand: In Learning, PO Box 1051, Springwood QLD, Brisbane, Australia 4127   Tel: 61-7-3-841-2286, Facsimile: 61-7-3-841-1580
ATTN: Messrs. Gordon

Singapore: 85, Genting Lane, Guan Hua Warehouse Bldng #05-01, Singapore 349569   Tel: 65-749-3389, Facsimile: 65-749-1129
ATTN: Evelyn Lee

Japan: Phoenix Associates Co., LTD., Mizuho Bldng. 3-F, 2-12-2, Kami Osaki, Shinagawa-Ku, Tokyo 141   Tel: 81-33-443-7231, Facsimile: 81-33-443-7640
ATTN: Mr. Peter Owans

CANADA

Reid Publishing, Ltd., Box 69559 109 Thomas Street, Oakville, Ontario Canada L6J 7R4.   Tel: (905) 842-4428, Facsimile: (905) 842-9327
ATTN: Mr. Stanley Reid

Trade Book Stores: *Raincoast Books*, 8680 Cambie Street, Vancouver, B.C., V6P 6M9   Tel: (604) 323-7100, Facsimile: (604) 323-2600
ATTN: Order Desk

EUROPEAN UNION

England: *Flex Training*, Ltd. 9-15 Hitchin Street, Baldock, Hertfordshire, SG7 6A, England   Tel: 44-1-46-289-6000, Facsimile: 44-1-46-289-2417
ATTN: Mr. David Willetts

INDIA

Multi-Media HRD, Pvt., Ltd., National House, Tulloch Road, Appolo Bunder, Bombay, India 400-039   Tel: 91-22-204-2281, Facsimile: 91-22-283-6478
ATTN: Messrs. Aggarwal

SOUTH AMERICA

Mexico: *Grupo Editorial Iberoamerica*, Nebraska 199, Col. Napoles, 03810 Mexico, D.F.   Tel: 525-523-0994, Facsimile: 525-543-1173
ATTN: Señor Nicholas Grepe

SOUTH AFRICA

Alternative Books, Unit A3 Micro Industrial Park, Hammer Avenue, Stridom Park, Randburg, 2194 South Africa   Tel: 27-11-792-7730, Facsimile: 27-11-792-7787
ATTN: Mr. Vernon de Haas